BICYCLE
POKER
OFFICIAL RULES AND GAMES

George White, Executive Editor
Erin Enzweiler, Editor

Transcontinental Printing
Canada

THE UNITED STATES PLAYING CARD COMPANY
Cincinnati, OH

ISBN: 1-889752-27-4

Transcontinental Printing Inc.
Printed in Canada

The United States Playing Card Company

4590 Beech St.
Cincinnati, OH 45212

Cover Design: Carrie E. Kepner

Acknowledgements:

We would like to thank the following contributors to this publication:

> Ray Doth
>
> Steve Schneider
>
> Geoff Wise
>
> Steve Tong
>
> Wyoming, OH, Friday Men's Poker Game
>
> The "If I Had a Quarter..." Poker Group

BICYCLE

Poker
Table of Contents

BICYCLE
I.

A Brief History of Playing Cards

Did you know that at one time, the king of hearts represented Charlemagne, the king of diamonds was Julius Caesar, the king of clubs was Alexander the Great, and the king of spades was King David from the Bible? These fascinating identities, along with special designations for the other "court cards" (the jack, queen and king), were bestowed by the French, who were instrumental in bringing the pleasures of card play to people in Europe and the New World.

The earliest playing cards are believed to have originated in Central Asia. The documented history of card playing began in the

10th century, when the Chinese began using paper dominoes by shuffling and dealing them in new games. Four-suited decks with court cards evolved in the Muslim world and were imported by Europeans before 1370. In those days, cards were hand-painted and only the very wealthy could afford them, but with the invention of woodcuts in the late 14th century, Europeans began mass-production of playing cards.

It is from French designs that the cards we use today are derived. France gave us the suits of spades, clubs, diamonds and hearts, and the use of simple shapes and flat colors helped facilitate manufacture. French cards soon flooded the market and were exported in all directions. They became the standard in England first, and then in the British Colonies of America.

Americans began making their own cards around 1800. Yankee ingenuity soon invented or adopted practical refinements: double-headed court cards (to avoid the nuisance of turning the figure upright), varnished surfaces (for durability and smoothness in shuffling), indexes (the identifying marks placed in the cards' borders or corners), and rounded corners (which avoid the wear that card players inflict on square corners).

Americans also invented the Joker. It originated around 1870 and was inscribed as the "Best Bower," the highest card in the game of Euchre. Since the game was sometimes called "Juker," it is thought that the Best Bower card might have been referred to as the "Juker card" which eventually evolved into "Joker." By the 1880s, certainly, the card had come to depict a jocular imp, jester or clown. Many other images were also used, especially as Jokers became vehicles for social satire and commercial advertising. Similarly, the backs of cards were used to promote ideas, products and services, and to depict famous landmarks, events — and even fads.

During this same period, cycling — on unicycles, bicycles, and tricycles — was taking the country by storm. It was also in the latter part of the 1880's that Russell & Morgan, the forerunners of The United States Playing Card Company, decided to produce a line of cards of the highest quality. Employees were asked to suggest an attractive name for the new product, and a printer, "Gus" Berens, offered "Bicycle." His idea was enthusiastically accepted, and the Bicycle Rider Back deck made its debut in 1887. Since then, while the Bicycle brand has featured dozens of additional, different designs, the Rider Back has never gone out of production.

Today, people all over the world are familiar with the traditional red or blue back showing cupid astride a two-wheeler. The Bicycle brand has become synonymous with quality and is still "America's Favorite Playing Cards™."

BICYCLE II.

Poker Introduction

As early as the 16th century, Germans played a bluffing game which they called "Pochen." It later developed into a French version, called "Poque," which was eventually brought over to New Orleans and played on the riverboats that plied the Mississippi.

In the 1830s, the game was refined further and became known as Poker. During the Civil War, the key rule about drawing cards to improve one's hand was added. A variation — Stud Poker — appeared at about the same time.

Today, Poker is truly an international game, enjoyed in virtually every country where card games are played. There are hundreds of versions of Poker, and the game is played not only in private homes, but also in countless Poker rooms at famous casinos. Poker can be played socially for pennies or match sticks, or professionally for thousands of dollars. There is plenty of luck in Poker, but the game requires great skill as well, and each player is the master of his own fate.

As with Backgammon and Gin Rummy, the luck-to-skill ratio is hard to quantify, but with games such as these, a novice can win in a short session; however, over the course of playing for many hours, the better player will invariably prevail. Herbert O. Yardley, who wrote the classic book *The Education of a Poker Player* in 1957, said that he never lost at more than three consecutive sessions. Indeed, if a player constantly loses in more sessions than he wins, then such a player is not just unlucky; he is simply being outplayed. With the exception of Bridge, Poker demands more skill than any other card game. Some people would debate even this statement and say that Poker stands at the very apex of card games requiring skill.

BICYCLE
1

General Rules That Apply to All Poker Games

Certain customs of card play are so well established that it is unnecessary to repeat them as part of the rules for every game, unless otherwise stated. The following rules can be assumed to apply to any Poker game, in the absence of any rule stating otherwise.

Number of Players

Poker may be played by two to 10 players, but most experienced players consider five to eight players ideal. Everyone plays for himself.

No two players may play in partnership, and there may be no agreement between two or more players to divide a pot.

The Pack

The standard 52-card pack, sometimes with the addition of one or two jokers as wild cards, is used. The pack consists of four suits: spades (♠), hearts (♥), diamonds (♦) and clubs (♣). In each suit there are 13 cards: **A, K, Q, J, 10, 9, 8, 7, 6, 5, 4, 3, 2.** Poker is a one-pack game, but today, in virtually all games played in clubs and among the best players, two packs of contrasting colors are utilized in order to speed up the game. While one pack is being dealt, the other is being shuffled and pre-pared for the next deal. The procedure for two packs is as follows: While the deal is in progress, the previous dealer assembles all the cards from the pack he dealt, shuffles them as many times as desired, and places them to the left. When it is time for the next deal, the shuf-fled deck is passed to the next dealer, who may shuffle them further, and then passes them to his left-hand opponent, who cuts the pack.

In clubs, it is customary to change cards often and to permit any player to call for new cards whenever he wishes. When new cards are introduced, both packs are replaced, and the seal and cellophane wrapping on the new decks should be broken in full view of all the players.

The Joker(s)

A fifty-third card–the joker–and a fifty-fourth card, which may be used as an extra joker, are usually furnished with the standard 52-card pack and may become part of the pack if the rules of the game require it. A number of versions of Poker, for example Pai-Gow, utilize one or both jokers.

Object of the Game

The goal of each player is to win the pot that contains all the bets that the players have made in any one deal. A player makes a bet in hopes that he has the best hand, or to give the impression that he does. In most Poker versions, the top combination of five cards is the best hand.

Seating

Players take seats at random unless any player requests before the game begins that the seats of the respective players be determined as provided in the next paragraph.

When any player requests a reseating, the banker has first choice of seats. The first dealer may either take the seat to the left of the banker or participate with the other players in having his position determined by chance as follows: the dealer shuffles the pack, has the cards cut by the player on his right and deals one card, face up, to each player, beginning with the player to his left. The player dealt the highest-ranking card sits to the right of the banker, the player with the next-highest card at the right of that player, and so on. If two players are dealt cards of the same rank, the card dealt first ranks higher.

After the game begins, no player may request a reseating unless at least one hour has elapsed since the last reseating. A player entering the game after it begins must take any vacant seat. A player replacing another player must take the seat that player vacated. Two players may exchange seats after any showdown and before the next deal begins, provided no other player objects. When there is no banker, the dealer has first choice of seats.

The Draw

There are several methods for determining the right to deal first. The most common method is as follows: the pack is shuffled and then spread face down on the table, with the cards overlapping. Each player draws one card, but none of the four cards at each end of the pack may be drawn. The person who draws the highest ranked card deals first. If two or more players draw cards of the same rank, everyone draws a new card since the suits are not ranked.

Rotation

The right to deal, the turn to bet, and the turn to play all rotate clockwise–that is, from each player to his left-hand neighbor.

The Shuffle

Any player at the table has the right to shuffle the pack (and as a matter of common practice, this right remains even where special rules of a game designate one player responsible for shuffling). In most games, the dealer has the right to shuffle last, and this is the rule when no different provision is stated.

The Cut

Cutting is the act of dividing the deck into two packets and transposing the bottom packet to the top. The custom is for the dealer to present the pack, after shuffling, to his right-hand neighbor, who lifts a packet from the top and sets it down beside the bottom packet. The dealer completes the cut by placing the bottom packet on top of the other. Each packet of the cut must contain a minimum of cards, which varies in different games, but is usually four or five. When two decks are being used to speed the game, the dealer's right-hand opponent shuffles the deck and the left-hand opponent then cuts the deck.

First Player

This term refers to the left-hand neighbor of the dealer. Although this term is not used in all games, and other equivalent terms are encountered (such as "First Hand"), the player in this position bets first in some games and plays first in most games.

The Deal

In most games, the first card dealt goes to the "first player," and the cards are distributed in clockwise rotation. The number of cards dealt at one time varies and is expressly stated for every game. The rule may be "one at a time," or "two at a time," or more at a time, but the same number of cards is dealt to every player in any one round. Sometimes the quota varies from round to round. For example, the rule to "deal 3-2" means, to deal a round of three cards at a time, then a round of two cards at a time. Unless otherwise noted, all cards must be dealt face down so that no player can see the face of a card dealt to another. If a card is found face up in the deck, it is usually a cause for declaring a misdeal.

Misdealing

It is a universal rule that when a player requests it, there must be a new deal by the same dealer if the customary or prescribed rules of shuffling, cutting, and dealing are breached in any way. Usually the request may no longer be made by a player who has looked at any of the cards dealt to him, or by any player after the prescribed deal has been completed, unless an irregular number of cards is found in a hand.

Incorrect Pack

A pack is incorrect if it does not comprise exactly the number, rank, and suits of cards prescribed by the rules of a specific game. A deck will be incorrect if some cards have been dropped on the floor or have been gathered up in another pack, or if the pack contains some cards belonging to another pack. If the pack is found to be incorrect, the current deal is abandoned at once, even though it may have progressed through various stages of bidding or play and all bets returned to each player. All games completed before that deal, however, stand without change.

Imperfect Pack

The term "imperfect" is used in a narrower sense, to mean an incorrect pack that cannot be rectified by the simple act of removing foreign cards or restoring cards that were originally included in it. The most common imperfection is when cards have become so worn and defaced that some are identifiable from the back. If a pack is found to be imperfect, but only through having an identifiable card, the current deal usually stands as if dealing has been completed, but the pack is then replaced prior to the next deal.

Wild Cards

A joker or any other card or class of cards may be designated as "wild" in a number of games by declaration of the dealer. Prior to play, players in the game must agree that wild cards may represent any other card that its holder does *not* have or any other card, whether or not the holder of the wild card also has the card designated. (This permits double- or even triple-ace-high flushes, and the like). A wild card, properly designated, ranks exactly the same as a natural card.

Rank of Cards

A (high) K, Q, J, 10, 9, 8, 7, 6, 5, 4, 3, 2. The ace may be low only in the sequence 5, 4, 3, 2, A if announced by the dealer prior to the deal. Optional: the ace may rank low in Low Poker (Lowball) or in High-Low Poker when, by agreement, the ace is designated as low. In Low Poker, the ace is always low, so that two aces is a lower pair than two 2s (deuces). In

High-Low Poker, the holder must designate the relative rank of the ace at the time that he shows his hand in the showdown, for example, by saying "aces high" (in which case two aces beats two kings for high), or "aces low" (in which case, two aces beats two 2s for low but loses to two 2s for high). In any pot to be won by the high hand, the ranking goes from ace down to two so that, for example, 7, 6, 4, 3, 2 beats 7, 5, 4, 3, 2.

Rank of Hands

While Poker is played in innumerable forms, a player who understands the values of the Poker hands and the principles of betting can play without difficulty in any type of Poker game. Except in a few versions of the game, a Poker hand consists of five cards. The various combinations of Poker hands rank from five of a kind (the highest) to "no pair" or "nothing" (the lowest):

Five of a Kind. This is the highest possible hand and can occur only in games where at least one card is wild. Examples of five of a kind would be four 10s and a wild card or two queens and three wild cards. In the event that two or more hands have five of a kind, the higher ranked card wins.

Straight Flush. This is the highest possible hand when there are no wild cards. A straight flush consists of five cards of the same suit in sequence, such as 10, 9, 8, 7, and 6 of hearts. The highest-ranking straight flush is the A, K, Q, J, and 10 of one suit, and this combination has a special name: a ***royal flush*** or a ***royal straight flush.*** The odds on being dealt this hand are 1 in almost 650,000. The lowest straight flush is 5, 4, 3, 2, A (if aces were announced as low) of the same suit. When there are two straight flushes in the same game, the one headed by the highest card wins. When any card has been designated as wild, a straight flush loses to five of a kind, which is the highest possible hand.

Four of a Kind. Four of a kind consists of four cards of the same rank. An example is four aces or four 3s. It does not matter what the fifth, unmatched card is. If two players have four of a kind, the four higher-ranking cards win. When there are wild cards, it is possible for two players to hold four of a kind of the same rank. In this case, the winning hand is the one with the higher-ranking fifth card.

Full House. This colorful hand is made up of three cards of one rank and two cards of another rank, such as three 8s and two 4s, or three aces and two 6s. When two hands each have a full house, the one with the higher-ranking three of a kind is the winner. When there are wild cards, two players may have full houses in which the three of a kind holdings are the same rank; the higher of the pairs then determines the winning hand. In event of a tie, the players split the pot.

Flush. Five cards all of the same suit, but not all in sequence, is a flush. An example is Q, 10, 7, 6, and 2 of clubs. If two players have a flush, the one containing the highest card wins. If the highest cards are the same rank, the higher of the next-highest cards determines the winning hand, and so on; so that A, K, 4, 3, 2 beats A, Q, J, 10, 8 and J, 9, 8, 6, 4 beats J, 9, 8, 6, 3.

Straight. Five cards in sequence, but not all of the same suit, is a straight. The ace is high in the straight A, K, Q, J, 10 and low in the straight 5, 4, 3, 2, A. If there are two or more straights, the one containing the highest card wins, so that 6, 5, 4, 3, 2 beats 5, 4, 3, 2, A.

12

Three of a Kind. This combination contains three cards of the same rank, and the other two cards each of a different rank, such as three jacks, a seven, and a four. If there are two or more hands each containing three of a kind, the one with the higher-ranking three of a kind wins. When there are wild cards, there may be two hands containing identical threes of a kind. In that case, the highest-ranking unmatched card determines the winner. If these cards are of the same rank, the higher-ranking fifth card in each hand determines the winner.

Two Pairs. This hand contains a pair of one rank and another pair of a different rank, plus any fifth card of a different rank, such as Q, Q, 7, 7, 4. If two or more hands each contain two pairs, the one with the highest pair wins. If the higher pairs are of the same rank, the one with the higher-ranking second pair wins. If these pairs are also of the same rank, the hand containing the higher of the unmatched cards is the winner.

One Pair. This frequent combination contains just one pair with the other three cards being of different rank. An example is 10, 10, K, 4, 3. If there are two or more one-pair hands, the one containing the higher pair wins. If two hands contain pairs of the same rank, the highest unmatched card determines the winner; if these are the same, the higher of the second-highest unmatched cards wins, and if these are the same, the higher of the lowest unmatched cards wins. For example, 8, 8, 9, 5, 3 beats 8, 8, 9, 5, 2.

No Pair. This very common hand contains "nothing." None of the five cards pair up, nor are all five cards of the same suit or consecutive in rank. When more than one player has no pair, the hands are rated by the highest card each hand contains, so that an ace-high hand beats a king-high hand, and so on.

Tie Hands. Two hands that are identical, card for card, are tied since the suits have no relative rank in Poker. In such a case, the tied players split the pot.

How the Betting Works

In the course of each Poker deal, there will be one or more betting intervals in which the players have an opportunity to bet on their hands. Betting is the key to Poker, for the game, in essence, is a game of chip management. Minimizing losses with poor hands and maximizing winnings with good hands is the underlying skill that Poker requires.

The Ante. The rules of the Poker game being played may require that each player put an equal amount of chips into the pot before any cards are dealt. This is called the ante. The amount of the ante is agreed upon before the game or is determined by the dealer.

Opening. After the deal, the beginning player (see "Sequence of Play" below) announces whether he will pass, bet, or fold (drop, or throw in his cards). If he passes and every player in turn, including the dealer, passes, there is a new deal by the next player on the left and the ante (if any) is repeated. If he bets, he is the first to bet, called "opening," and puts the number of chips he is betting into the pot. Each player to the left, in turn, must either "call" that bet by putting into the pot the same number of chips; or "raise," which means that he puts in enough chips to call and then makes an additional bet; or "fold" ("drop"), which means that he puts no chips in the pot, discards his hand, and is out of the betting until the next deal. When a player folds, he loses any chips he has put into that pot. Unless a player is willing to put into the pot at least as many

15

chips as any preceding player, he must drop out (fold).

Sequence of Play. In each betting interval, the turn to bet begins with the player designated by the rules of the Poker version being played and moves to each active player on the left. No player may open, check, call, raise, or fold, except in his proper turn. A player may neither pass nor bet until the player on his right has checked, put the correct number of chips into the pot, or has folded. In Draw Poker, the first in turn before the draw is the player on the dealer's left. The first in turn after the draw is the player who made the first bet before the draw or, if he has dropped, the player on his left. In Stud Poker, the first in each betting interval is the player whose exposed cards are higher than those of any other player. If two or more players have identical high holdings, the player with the highest holding closest to the dealer's left is first. If a player wishes to remain in the game without betting, he "checks." This means, in effect, that the player is making a "bet of nothing." A player may check provided no one before him in that betting interval has made a bet. If another player has bet, he cannot check but must at least call the bet or fold. A player who checks may

16

subsequently raise a bet that has been raised by another player. This is called "sandbagging," which is allowed, unless it has been decided beforehand that this practice is forbidden. If all players check during a round of play, the betting interval is over, and all the players still in the pot remain in the game. If a player makes a bet or a raise that no other player calls, he wins the pot without showing his hand. Thus, in Poker, there is a bluffing element, and the best combination of cards does not always win the pot! Bluffing is one of the key reasons why Poker is so popular.

Call. A call is a bet equal to the previous bet, that is, a matching number of chips. This amount must include any raises made during this betting interval. For example, a bet of five is "called" by the next player (also "betting five"); the next player "raises" two (bets a total of seven, matching the previous bet of five and adding two more). Any bet by the next player must be seven to call (matching the previous bets of five and two) or more than seven to raise.

Raise. A raise is a bet greater than the previous bet.

Fold or Drop. A player in turn may fold even when he has the privilege of checking. Any time that a player discards his hand, or permits it to be mixed with any discard, he has folded, and his hand may not be reclaimed.

The Showdown. Depending on the version of Poker being played, after all cards have been dealt and each player has either called the highest previous bet without raising or has folded, or when every active player has checked, the full hand of every active player is placed face up on the table, and the highest-ranking hand wins the pot. If two or more hands tie for the highest rank, they divide the pot evenly, any odd chip going to the player who last bet or raised. It is customary for a player to announce the value of his hand. When there are wild cards, he must announce the value of his hand and may then claim no higher hand. Whenever only one active player remains because all other players have dropped, the remaining player wins the pot without showing his hand, and there is a new deal by the next dealer in turn.

Knowing When to Bet

The ranking of Poker hands is based on mathematics. The less likely a player is to get a certain hand, the higher it ranks and the more likely it is to win the pot. For example, a player in Five-Card Stud Poker should not expect to be dealt a straight flush more than once in 65,000 hands, but he can expect to be dealt two pair about once in every 21 hands. Unless a player is planning to bluff, he should not make a bet without holding a hand that he thinks may be the best. No Poker player can bet intelligently unless he knows what constitutes a good hand, a fair hand, and a bad hand. The odds of being dealt each type of Poker hand in five-card stud are as follows:

Royal Flush: 1:650,000
Straight Flush: 1:65,000
Four of a Kind: 1:4,000
Full House: 1:700
Flush: 1:500
Straight: 1:250
Three of a Kind: 1:50
Two pair: 1:20
One Pair: 1:2.33

Betting Limits

There are different ways of fixing a betting limit. Some limit is necessary; otherwise a player with a lot more money would have, or would be perceived to have, an unfair advantage. Once fixed, the limit should be unalterable throughout the game unless the players unanimously agree to change the stakes. Some popular limit systems follow:

Fixed limit. No one may bet or raise by more than a stipulated number of chips, for example, two, or five, or 10. Usually this limit varies with the stage of the game: In Draw Poker, if the limit is five before the draw, it might be ten after the draw. In Stud Poker, if the limit is five in the first four betting intervals, it is ten in the final betting interval (and often ten whenever a player has a pair or better showing).

Pot limit. Any bet or raise is limited to the number of chips in the pot at that time. This means that a player who raises may count as part of the pot the number of chips required for him to call. If there are six chips in the pot, and a bet of four is made, the total is 10 chips; it requires four chips for the next player to call, making 14; and the player may then raise by 14 chips. However, even when the pot limit is played, there should be some maximum limit, such as 50 chips.

Table stakes. The limit for each player is the number of chips the player has in front of him. If the player has only 10 chips, he may bet no more than 10 and he may call any other player's bet to that extent. In table stakes, no player may withdraw chips from the table, or return chips to the banker, until he leaves the game. A player may add to his stack, but only between the deal just completed and the beginning of the next deal.

Whangdoodles, or Roodles. In a fixed-limit game, it is often agreed that following any very good hand — a full house or better, for example — there will be one deal by each player of Jacks or Better, in which everyone antes double, and the betting limit is doubled for these deals as well.

Poverty Poker. A maximum limit is put on the number of chips any player may lose. Each takes out one stack at the start; if he loses that stack, the banker issues the player another, without charging for it, and in many cases, the player can get still a third stack free before dropping out of the game. (Some limit should be placed on the number of free stacks so that a player will have the incentive to play carefully.)

No limit. In these sessions, the "sky's the limit," but such games are rarely played today.

Limits on the Number of Raises

In almost all games played today, there is a limit on the number of raises at each betting interval, and this limit is invariably three raises.

The Kitty

By unanimous or majority agreement, the players may establish a special fund called a "kitty." Usually the kitty is built up by "cutting" (taking) one low-denomination chip from each pot in which there is more than one raise. The kitty belongs to all the players equally, and it is used to pay for new decks of cards or for food and drinks. Any chips left in the kitty when the game ends are divided equally among the players who are still in the game. Unlike the rule in some other games, such as Pinochle, when a player leaves a Poker game before it ends, he is not entitled to take his share of chips that comprised part of the kitty.

Chips

Poker is almost always played with poker chips. For a game with seven or more players, there should be a supply of at least 200 chips. Usually, the white chip (or the lightest-colored chip) is the unit, or lowest-valued chip, worth whatever the minimum ante or bet is; a red chip (or some other colored chip) is worth five whites, and a blue chip (or some other dark-colored chip) is worth 10 or 20 or 25 whites or two, four or five reds. At the start of the game, each player "buys in" by purchasing a certain number of chips. All of the players usually buy in for the same amount.

Banker

One player should be designated as the banker, who keeps the stock of chips and records how many have been issued to each player or how much cash the player has paid for his chips. Players should make no private transactions or exchanges among themselves; a player with surplus chips may return them to the banker and receive credit or cash for them, while a player who wants more chips should obtain them only from the banker.

Irregularities

Redeal. Any player, unless he has intentionally seen the face of any card dealt to him face down, may call for a new shuffle, cut, and deal by the same dealer if, before the dealer begins dealing the second round of cards:

1) A card was exposed in cutting.

2) The cut left fewer than five cards in either packet.

3) Two or more cards are face up in the pack.

4) The pack is incorrect or imperfect in any way.

5) A player is dealing out of turn.

If a player is dealing out of turn, and a redeal is called, the deal reverts to the proper player in turn. In a game in which every player antes, no one need ante again. Any other bet is left in the pot. If no redeal or misdeal is called within a time limit provided, the deal stands, and the player on the left of the out-of-turn dealer will be the next dealer.

Misdeal. A misdeal due to the dealer's error loses the deal if attention is drawn to it by a player who has not intentionally seen any face-down card dealt to him. The deal passes to the next player in turn. The misdealer's ante is forfeited to the pot. If all players have anted equally, their antes remain in the pot and no one need ante again. A blind bet or raise may be withdrawn.

A misdeal may be called by any player who has not intentionally seen any face-down card dealt to him:

    1) If before the dealer begins the second round of cards he notices that the pack was not shuffled or offered for cut.

    2) By any player who receives two face-up cards in Draw Poker or any other form of closed Poker, provided he calls a mis deal immediately and has not contributed to the error.

    3) If the dealer gives too many cards to more than one player.

If the dealer mistakenly stops dealing before giving every player enough cards, due solely to his omission to deal one or more rounds, it is not a misdeal and the dealer is required to complete the deal whenever the irregularity is discovered. For example, if the dealer stops dealing after giving each player only four cards; or if the dealer gives the first five of seven players five cards each and the sixth and seventh players only four cards each, it is not a misdeal. If the dealer deals too many hands, he shall determine which hand is dead, and that hand is discarded; but if any player has looked at any face-down card in any hand, he must keep that hand. If the dealer deals too few hands, he must give his hand to the first omitted player to his left. Any other player who has been omitted and who has anted may withdraw his ante.

Exposed Card. If the dealer exposes one or more cards from the undealt portion of the pack after the deal is completed, those cards are dead and are placed among the discards. There is no penalty against any player for exposing any part of his hand, and he has no redress. A player who interferes with the deal and causes the dealer to expose a card may not call a misdeal.

Incorrect Pack. If it is determined, at any time before the pot has been taken in, that the pack has too many cards, too few cards, or duplicate cards, the deal is void; and each player withdraws from the pot any chips he contributed to it, any other laws of the game to the contrary notwithstanding; but the results of pots previously taken in are not affected.

Imperfect Pack. If the pack contains any card that is torn, discolored, or otherwise marked so it can be identified from the back, the pack must be replaced before the deal in progress or any other deal can be completed; but the play of the hand in progress is not affected if the deal has been completed.

Incorrect Hand. A hand having more or less than the correct number of cards in the Poker variation being played is foul and cannot win the pot. If every other player has dropped, the pot remains and goes to the winner of the next pot. Players may agree that a hand with fewer cards is not foul, in which case its holder may compete for the pot with the best Poker combination he can make.

Irregularities in Betting. Chips once put in the pot may not be withdrawn except by a player who, after he has anted, is dealt out; or in Jacks or Better, when another player has opened without proper openers (see Laws of Draw Poker); in Draw Poker, by the players who opened or raised blind, in case of a misdeal; or in Stud Poker, when the dealer has failed to deal a player any card face down.

Installment or String Bets. A player's entire bet must be put in the pot at one time. Having put in some number of chips, he may not add to that number unless the original number was insufficient to call, in which case he may add exactly enough chips to call. If, however, he announced before putting in any chips that he was raising by a certain amount and puts in an amount insufficient for such a raise, he must on demand supply enough additional chips to equal the announced amount of his bet.

Insufficient Bet. When a player in turn puts into the pot a number of chips insufficient to call, he must either add enough chips to call and may not raise, or he must drop and forfeit his chips already in the pot. When a player raises by less than the minimum permitted, he is deemed to have called, and any additional chips he put into the pot are forfeited to it.

Bet Above Limit. If a player puts in the pot more chips than are permitted by the limit, it stands as a bet of the limit and additional chips are forfeited to the pot. An exception is made in table stakes when a player's bet exceeds the number of chips an opponent has. In that event, the player may withdraw the excess and either bet it in a side pot, or, if no other players are willing or able to meet that bet in the side pot, restore those chips to his stack.

Announcement in Turn of Intention to Pass or Bet. If a player in turn announces that he passes or folds, his announcement is binding whether or not he discards his hand. If a player in turn announces a bet but does not put any chips in the pot, he is bound by his announcement and must, if possible, supply additional chips necessary to bring the bet up to the announced amount.

Announcement Out of Turn of Intention to Pass or Bet. If a player out of turn announces his intention to pass or fold when his turn comes, and then, does not actually discard his hand, or to make a certain bet but does not actually put any chips in the pot, his announcement is void; and he may take any action he chooses when his turn comes. Any other player who acts in reliance upon the out-of-turn announcement does so at his own risk and has no redress.

Bet Out of Turn. If a player puts any chips in the pot out of turn, they remain there, and the play reverts to the player whose turn it was. If any player to the offender's left puts chips in the pot, he has bet out of turn and is equally an offender. When the offender's turn comes, if the chips he put in were insufficient to call, the player may add enough chips to call. If the amount was exactly sufficient to call, he is deemed to have called. If the amount was more than enough to call, the player is deemed to have raised by the amount of the excess but cannot add chips to increase the amount of his raise. If no player before him has bet, he is deemed to have bet the number of chips he put in and any amount above the agreed limit is forfeited to the pot. If the chips he put in were insufficient to call, he may forfeit these chips and fold. However, the player may never add chips to raise or to increase his raise.

Pass Out of Turn. The pass (act of folding) out of turn is among the most damaging of Poker improprieties, but there is no penalty except by prior agreement of the players. In any case, the offender's hand is dead and he cannot win the pot.

Irregularities in the Showdown. If a player in the showdown announces a hand he does not actually hold, the announcement is void if the error is discovered before the pot has been taken in by any player (including the player who miscalled his hand). "The cards speak for themselves."

Designation of Wild Cards. If, in the showdown, a player orally designates the suit or rank of a wild card in his hand, or implies such designation by announcing a certain hand, he may not change that designation (for example, an announcement of joker J, 10, 9, 8 as "jack-high straight" fixes the joker as a seven). A player may always show his hand without announcement and need not designate the value of a wild card unless another active player requests that he do so.

Concession of a Pot. A player who has discarded his hand after another player's announcement of a higher hand may not later claim the pot — even if the announcement was incorrect.

32

BICYCLE
2

Draw Poker and Stud Poker General Facts

The main forms of Poker are Draw Poker and Stud Poker. In Draw Poker, all the cards are dealt face down to the players.

In Stud Poker, some of the cards are dealt face up as the betting progresses, so that all of the other players get to see a part of each player's hand. Unless the host, or the rule of a club, has already established the game, the players should first decide what form of Poker they will play. Two factors should influence their decision: the number of players, and whether the group has only experienced players or has some inexperienced players.

The following selections are recommended:

Two, three, or four players. Stud Poker in any form. Usually, with so few players, only the very experienced play Draw Poker and they will often use a stripped deck, which is a pack with cards removed, such as all the deuces (twos) and treys (threes).

Five to eight players. Any form of Poker, either Draw or Stud.

Nine or ten players. Five-Card Stud Poker.

More than 10 players. One of the games in which fewer than five cards are dealt, such as Three-Card Monte or Spit-in-the-Ocean. All of the Poker variations are described later in this chapter. Another alternative with so many players is to simply form two tables and organize two separate games.

Dealer's Choice

When the Poker session is Dealer's Choice, each dealer has the privilege of naming the form of Poker to be played and to designate the ante, wild cards (if any), and the maximum limit of chips that can be wagered during each round. However, the dealer may not require one player to ante more than another. If a game such as Jacks or Better is selected and no one opens the betting, the same dealer deals again and everyone antes again.

Wild Cards

While most Poker purists choose to play with no wild cards, in many games, especially Dealer's Choice, various cards may be designated as wild. A wild card is specified by the holder to be a card of any rank or suit, such as a fifth queen, or the card needed to combine with the other four in a player's hand to form a straight or a flush. Wild cards in a Poker game add variety, and of course, they greatly increase the chances of getting a rare combination such as a full house or a straight flush. The usual choices for wild cards are as follows:

The joker. Note that most packs of cards include two jokers for use in such games as Canasta. Poker players are increasingly adding one or both jokers as wild cards.

The bug. This is the joker, but its wildness is limited: It counts as an ace; or as a card of any suit for making a flush; or as a card of any rank and suit for making a straight or straight flush. It may not be used as an additional card to make three of a kind or four of a kind, except as an ace.

Deuces. "Deuces Wild" is a popular form of Draw Poker. Every two is wild. Sometimes one or two jokers are included as additional wild cards. Note that the number of wild cards in a hand does not diminish it in any way; thus, with deuces wild, five of a kind comprised of 10, 10, 2, 2, 2 (five 10s) beats 8, 8, 8, 8, 2 (five 8s).

One-eyed cards. The king of diamonds and the jacks of spades and hearts show only one eye, whereas the other face cards each have two eyes. One-eyed jacks are sometimes designated as wild cards, but the king of diamonds (sometimes called the "man with the axe") is rarely selected to be wild.

Suicide King. The king of hearts is sometimes designated as a wild card.

Low hole card. In the game of Stud Poker, each player's lowest "hole" card (that is, the lowest card that is dealt face down and not seen by the other players) can be designated as wild. In Draw Poker, the wild card would be the lowest card in a player's hand. When such a card is designated, it means that every card of that rank in that player's hand is wild, but the fact that a certain card is wild in one player's hand does not make that same rank of card wild in other players' hands.

Laws and Ethics

In every game, a written code of Poker laws should be used as the final judge for settling all questions. No Poker laws are universally followed — there are many local customs and preferences — but the Poker laws in this book embrace the latest customs of the most expert games and are recommended for adoption. It is a tradition of Poker that any club or group of players may make special rules, called "house rules," to suit their personal preferences. Of course, any such house rules should be written down.

Time Limit

Before play begins, the players should set a time limit for when the game ends and stick to it. Violation of this principle could eventually turn pleasant sessions into unpleasant ones. Often when the time for quitting is approaching, the host or one of the players will announce "one more round of deals" (everyone at the table deals one more hand) so that players will know how many deals are left and can gauge their strategies accordingly.

BICYCLE
3

Draw Poker

Principal Forms

There are several methods of playing Draw Poker, and they differ mostly in the rules governing betting. The essential features of the game, common to all varieties, are as follows:

Each player is dealt five cards face down, one at a time in rotation, beginning on the dealer's left. After the deal, there is a betting interval. The player on the dealer's left has the first right or obligation to bet. When the first betting interval has ended, each active player in turn, beginning with the player on the dealer's left, may discard one or more cards, and the dealer then gives him, from the top of the undealt portion of the pack, face down, as many cards as he discarded. This is the draw. A player may, if desired, "stand pat" (draw no cards). Unless otherwise stated, the maximum number of cards a player may draw is three or, if the player shows an ace to all the other players, he may draw four. (In some games, especially in casinos, a player may draw four cards without exposing an ace, or may draw five cards - a fresh hand.) Note that, unlike some other card games, the player must always discard before taking any new cards for his draw. After the draw, there is another betting interval, initiated by the player who made the first bet before the draw or, if he has dropped, the player on his left, followed by a showdown.

All games of Draw Poker fall into one of two classes, depending on the betting rules:

Pass and Out. Also called "Pass Out" or "Bet or Drop". In this method, whenever it is a player's turn, and if there has been no bet before him, he must bet the minimum allowed or fold. In most games, this rule applies only before the draw. After the draw, a player may check. In some games, however, each player must bet or fold before and after the draw.

This procedure is followed in casinos where the House runs the game.

Pass and Back In. At his first turn, a player may pass (check) rather than bet, provided no previous player has made a bet. The first player to make a bet is said to open. Once the pot is opened, each player in turn has another chance to stay in or drop out. After the draw, a player may check. This procedure is common in home games and other social games, and is the one used in the versions of Poker explained later in this book.

The Ante

The players must decide in advance which of two methods they will adopt for the ante: Either each player antes one chip before the deal or the dealer antes one chip for each of the players in the game before dealing. Thus, if there are six players in all, the dealer's ante is six chips.

Special Hands

To create more playable hands and enliven the game, many players give special value to one or more hands that are not among the traditional Poker hands. Players must agree in advance to include such hands in a game.

Skip straight (also called Dutch straight or Kilter). Five cards in an alternate sequence, such as Q, 10, 8, 6, 4, or K, J, 9, 7, 5. This hand beats three of a kind but loses to a straight.

Round-the-corner straight. A sequence such as 3, 2, A, K, Q. Note that the hand 5, 4, 3, 2, A beats 4, 3, 2, A, K, which beats 3, 2, A, K, Q, and so on. When both skip straights and round-the-corner straights are played, the skip straight ranks higher.

Fourflush. Four cards of the same suit and one card of another suit, not in sequence. A fourflush beats a pair, but loses to two pair.

Bobtail. A four-card straight in sequence with "both ends open." An example is 8, 7, 6, 5, with the fifth card not in sequence; A, K, Q, J is not a bobtail, because only a single card, the 10, will fill it; 9, 8, 6, 5 is not, because only a 7 will fill it. The bobtail beats a pair but loses to two pair. When bobtails and fourflushes are played, the latter beats the former.

Standard Draw Poker

This game is played as described beginning on page 39, and the player who makes the first bet does not need any minimum hand in order to bet. In other words, he can open the betting without even a pair. Once the betting round is complete and players have drawn their cards, the second betting round begins and all players who have not folded have the opportunity to bet again.

Some players vary this game slightly by playing a "blind opening," whereby the first hand must open the pot (or fold) and (usually) the next player must raise (or fold). This game is played "pass and out" (described above) before the draw, but usually "pass and back in" after the draw. This is the form of Poker played in private clubs when Draw Poker is selected instead of Stud. A variant of the blind opening is English or Australian Poker, in which a player who raises can double the preceding bet. (Raising in this game is often called "doubling".)

Rules of Draw Poker

The Draw. After each player has exactly called the highest previous bet without raising or has folded, the first betting interval ends. The dealer picks up the undealt portion of the pack, and each active player beginning on his left may, in turn, discard one or more cards. Then, the dealer gives him that number of cards, face down, from the top of the pack. A player need not draw unless he so chooses.

If the dealer is an active player, he must announce how many cards, if any, he is drawing. At any time following the draw and before the first player in turn bets or checks in the final betting interval, any active player may ask any other active player how many cards he drew. The latter player must answer, but the questioner has no redress if the answer is incorrect. It is considered unethical, however, to give an incorrect answer intentionally.

The dealer may not deal the bottom card of the pack. If the pack exclusive of this card does not suffice for the draw, the dealer assembles all cards previously discarded, plus the bottom card of the original pack, shuffles these cards, and offers them for a cut. Then, he continues dealing. The cut is described in "The

Shuffle and Cut" (on pages 5-6) except that only an active player may cut. The opener's discards and the discards of any player yet to draw are excluded from the reassembled pack if they have been kept separate and can be identified.

Irregularities.
Wrong number of cards. If the dealer gives a player more or fewer cards than he asks for, the error must be corrected if the player calls attention to it before he has looked at any of the cards. Unless a card has been served to the next active player in turn, the dealer must correct the error by supplying the missing cards or restoring the excess to the top of the pack, as the case may be. If the next player has been served, the player with the incorrect hand may discard the surplus cards. If he has already discarded and the draw is insufficient to restore his hand to five cards, his hand is foul. If the player has looked at any card of the draw and the entire draw would give him an incorrect number of cards, his hand is foul.

Exposed card. If any card is exposed in the draw, whether or not it was faced in the pack, the player must accept the first such card, but any additional exposed card is dead and is placed among the discards. After the dealer has served all other active players, he deals any additional cards due from the top of the pack.

Draw out of turn. If a player allows a player on his left to draw out of turn, he must play without drawing, or fold. If he has already discarded any card, his hand is foul. A player may correct a slip of the tongue in stating the number of cards he wishes to draw, but only if the dealer has not yet given the player the number of cards he first requested.

If a player discards a number of cards that would make his hand incorrect after the dealer gives him as many cards as he asked for, his hand is foul.

Showing openers. The player who opens must prove that he held a legal hand of five cards including the strength (if any) required to open. If the player is in the showdown, he must show his entire hand face up. In any other case, before discarding his entire hand, he must show his openers face up and his remaining cards, if any, face down.

Splitting openers. The player who opened may split his openers (discard one or more cards essential to them) and need not announce that

46

he is doing so. He may put his discard in the pot, face down, for reference later. For example, having opened with Q, Q, J, 10, 9, he may discard the Q and draw one card.

False openers. If it is determined at any time that a player opened without proper openers, or that his hand contains too many cards, the player's hand is foul, and all chips he has bet are forfeited to the pot. If false openers are discovered before the draw, any other player in turn to the offender's left (excluding those who passed in their first turns) may open. Play continues, but any player except the offender may withdraw from the pot any chips he put in after the pot was falsely opened. If no one can open, the rest of the pot remains for the next deal. If false openers are discovered after every player but the offender has dropped, the other players may withdraw from the pot any chips they put in after the pot was falsely opened. If false openers are discovered after the draw, and if any player remains active, play continues; and the pot goes to the highest hand at the showdown, whether or not any player had openers. (If there is no hand at the showdown that is not foul, the pot remains and goes to the winner of the next pot. Regardless of other circumstances, a hand that has dropped can never win a pot.)

48

BICYCLE
4
Stud Poker

In Stud Poker, each player is dealt one or more hole cards, face down. The remainder of his cards are dealt face up, with the exception of the last card, which may be dealt face down in some games. The two most popular standard Stud Poker games are Five-Card Stud and Seven-Card Stud. In Five-Card Stud, each player receives one card down and four subsequent cards up. In Seven-Card Stud, each player receives the first two cards down, four subsequent cards up and the last card down, although in some games the last card may be dealt up. After each player is dealt one card face up (an "up card"), and after each subsequent deal, there is a betting interval before dealing is resumed. Stud Poker has cut into the popularity of Draw Poker because there are more betting rounds (and thus, bigger pots), and there is a fascination about seeing some of the opponents' cards and trying to fathom what the hole card or cards may be.

Rules of Stud Poker

Incomplete hands. For the purpose of establishing the first bettor in any interval, exposed cards rank from highest to lowest as follows:

Four of a kind: Between two such hands, the four higher-ranking cards are high.

Three of a kind: If there are two such hands, the higher-ranking three of a kind is high.

Two pair: When two such combinations are showing, the highest pair determines the high hand, and if the highest pairs are the same, the higher of the two lower pairs.

One pair: Between two such hands, the higher pair is high. If two hands have the identical pair, the highest unmatched card determines the high hand, and if these are identical, the higher of the two other cards.

The highest card: If two players tie for highest card, the next-highest card in their respective hands determines the high hand, and so on.

If there are two holdings that are identical card for card, the one nearest the dealer's left is high for purposes of betting but has no superiority over the other holding in the showdown.

Flush and straight combinations of four or fewer cards rank no higher, for determining the first bettor, than any other holdings. This includes no pair except when a fourflush (four cards of the same suit) and/or a bobtail (a four-card straight) is played to beat a pair; in that case a fourflush showing bets ahead of a bobtail, which bets ahead of a pair.

If, through the dealer's or his own error, all a player's cards are exposed, all are taken into consideration for establishing the first bettor. If, at the start of the final betting interval, that player has a straight, flush, full house, or straight flush showing, his hand outranks any combination of exposed cards that it would beat in a showdown.

Irregularities.

At any time before the dealer begins dealing the second round of cards, a player who has not looked at a card dealt face down to him may call for a new shuffle, cut, and deal if the player notices that:

1) The pack was not shuffled or cut.

2) A card was exposed in cutting, or the cut left fewer than five cards in either packet.

3) Two or more cards are face up in the pack.

4) The pack is incorrect or imperfect in any way.

5) A player is dealing out of turn. When there is a redeal, the same dealer deals again unless he was dealing out of turn, in which case the deal reverts to the proper player.

If the dealer deals too many hands, he shall determine which hand is dead and that hand is discarded.

However, if a player has looked at the hole card of any hand, he must keep that hand.

If the dealer deals too few hands, he must give his own hand to the first omitted player to his left.

If the dealer gives a player two face-down cards instead of one during the first round of dealing, he turns up one of the cards and then omits that player on the second round of dealing (unless the rules of the game require two hole cards, as in Seven-Card Stud). The player who received the two cards may not look at them and then turn one of them up.

If the dealer gives a player more than two cards on the first deal, that player may require a redeal before the second round begins. If the error is not noted until later, his hand is dead.

If, in dealing any round of face-up cards, the dealer omits a player, he moves the cards one place backwards, so as to give each player the face-up card he would have had if no error had been made. However, if the error is not noticed before the first bet is made, the hand of the player who was omitted is dead.

Exposed card. If the dealer gives any player a hole card face up, the player must keep that card and receive his next card face down. The player has no redress, except to receive his next card face down, unless the dealer repeatedly fails to correct the error until the player has four cards. At that point, if the dealer has never given him a face-down card, the player may drop out and withdraw all his chips from the pot. If the player stays for his fifth card, and the fifth card is dealt face up, the player may withdraw his chips from the pot or may remain in the game and play with an exposed hand.

Dead cards. A card found face up in the pack during a round of dealing must be dealt to the appropriate player. If a card at the top of the pack is exposed during a betting interval, either because it is face up in the pack or prematurely dealt, it is discarded. In dealing the next round of face-up cards, the dealer skips the player who would have received that card and deals in rotation, ending with the player who would have received the exposed card. In each subsequent round, the dealer deals in the normal rotation.

Impossible call. If the last player to speak in the final betting interval calls a bet when his five cards (whatever his hole card may be) cannot possibly beat the four showing cards of the player whose bet he calls, the call is void and the chips may be retracted, provided that a player calls attention to the error before the hole card of any other active player is shown.

Error in Valuing the Hand. If the dealer errs in calling the value of a hand or in designating the high hand, no player has any redress. If the player incorrectly designated makes the first bet, it is not a bet out of turn.

Hole Card Irregularity. The dealer does not have the option of dealing a player's first card up and his second card down intentionally. A player may not turn up his hole card and receive his next card face down. If he turns up his hole card, he must play the round with his cards exposed.

BICYCLE
5

High-Low Poker

The basic idea of High-Low Poker is that the best Poker hand and the worst Poker hand split the pot. The original purpose of High-Low was to give holders of poor cards a chance to play. The game was found to be so enjoyable that it now rivals regular Poker in popularity, and it is a staple in Poker clubs and gambling casinos having a Poker room.

Forms of High-Low

Any form of Poker may be played high-low, whether or not there are wild cards, but the most popular version for high-low games is

Seven-Card Stud. In a high-low game, there are usually two winners, the player with the highest hand taking half the pot and the player with the lowest hand taking the other half. The high hand takes the odd chip if the pot will not divide evenly. In some cases there may be a single winner, as that player wins both the high hand and low hand (see explanation below).

Declarations

Some people play a version of High-Low that includes declaring whether they are trying for high, for low, or for both. After the final betting interval, but before the showdown, each player must declare what he is trying for. There are various methods of declaring, and the players should agree in advance which will be used. The most common method is that before any hands are shown, each player decides mentally what he is trying for. If the player decides upon low, he places one chip in his hand without letting the other players see it. He places two chips in his hand if he opts for high, and three chips if he is going for both high and low. When all players have "declared" (decided), they open their hands to reveal how many chips they are holding. If all players have decided the same way; the best hand in that category takes the whole pot.

When playing for both high and low, a player mentally selects two five-card hands from among the cards that he holds. (This is the one exception to discarding two cards in Seven-Card Stud prior to the showdown.) There are two ways in which tied hands may be ruled, but before the game, the dealer must announce which way the game will be played. The first version states that if a player claims both high and low, and is tied or beaten on either, he loses any title to the pot. The second version states that if a player declares both high and low, he must at least tie each way or he receives nothing.

Rank of Low Hands

When straights and flushes do not count, as in Lowball, the lowest hand is 5, 4, 3, 2, A. However, in some high-low games, the ace is always ranked highest, and flushes and straights do count and would interfere with the low hand. In such a case, 7, 5, 4, 3, 2 would be the lowest possible hand as long as all five cards were not of the same suit. It is very important for players to agree on what the lowest hand will be in High-Low. It is strongly recommended to allow aces to be high or low and for flushes and straights not to count for low hand. Thus, the wheel or bicycle (5, 4, 3, 2, A) would be the lowest possible hand.

With wild cards in a high-low game, any wild card ranks as a "zero", and the lowest hand would be 4, 3, 2, A, "0" in a game where, if there had been no wild cards allowed, the wheel would ordinarily be the lowest hand. Again, it is necessary for players to agree on what the lowest hand will be before play begins. Many experienced players agree that wild cards are best suited for high-hand games only, rather than for games of Lowball or High-Low.

High-Low - Eight or Better

In this version, played in Poker parlors and some home games, a qualifier of eight or better is needed for a player to be in contention for the low half of the pot. That is, a player cannot declare for the low hand unless he has a hand no higher than 8, 7, 6, 5, 3.

BICYCLE
6

Draw Poker Games

Of the many variations of Draw Poker, the basic rules for which are defined on pages 39-48, following are currently the most popular variants.

Joker Wild

In this Five-Card Draw game, one joker is added to the deck as a wild card and may represent any card. Five of a kind becomes the top hand and takes precedence over a Royal Flush. A joker can also stand for a duplicate ace, beating out another's Ace-high Flush.

This game can also be played with two jokers, making it Double Joker Wild.

One-Eyed Jacks

In this Five-Card Draw game, "One-Eyed Jacks" (Hearts and Spades) are wild. The player can use these cards to represent any card.

Jacks or Better (also known as Jackpots)

Once all players have placed their antes and the deal is completed, each player in turn has the right to "open" (make the first bet) but may not do so unless he has a pair of jacks or better. If no one opens (that is, every player passes), everyone antes again, and the same dealer deals again. (In some games, the deal passes to the left, even when no one opens.) If any player opens, the first betting interval has begun. Each other player in turn after him (including players who passed on the first round) must drop, call, or raise, until this betting interval ends. The game then continues as in standard Draw Poker.

In Jacks or Better, the player who opens must "show openers" before he can discard his hand. He need show only as many cards as will prove to the other players that he had the requirements. Of course, if this player is in the showdown, he must show his entire hand.

Jacks or Better Progressive

This is the same as Jacks or Better, except that if no one can open with jacks or better on the first deal, on the next deal queens or better are required to open. If two deals in a row are passed out and no one can open, kings or better are required, then aces or better. In some games, players will progress all the way up to two pair or better. Alternatively, they can return to jacks or better after aces or better.

Jacks or Bobtail to Open

Many players use a rule that the first player may open either on a pair of jacks or better, or on any Bobtail, which is an outside straight draw such as 10-9-8-7, that can be filled by either of two card ranks.

Jacks or Fourflush to Open

This is the same as Jacks or Better, but players may open with a Fourflush (four cards of the same suit and a fifth card of another suit) or a pair of jacks or better.

Jacks or Better, Deuces Wild

This is a regular game of Jacks or Better, but with all four deuces wild. Naturally, Deuces Wild can be played in virtually any Poker version, but it is most common in the game of Jacks or Better.

Aces or Better

A pair of aces or better is required to open.

Aces or Better Regressive

Players need a pair of aces or better to open on the first deal. On the next deal, it goes to kings or better. This continues down to jacks and then stays at jacks.

Double Draw

This version is the same as Standard Draw Poker, except it features a second draw after the second betting round, and then there is a third (final) betting round. For each draw, players are allowed up to three cards (holding an ace does not entitle the holder to draw four cards). Obviously, because of the extra betting round, the pots will be bigger, and with two draws, the final hands of the players will invariably be better.

Shotgun

Three cards are dealt to each player face down and there is a round of betting. Other rounds of betting follow the dealing of the fourth and fifth cards. Players still in the game then draw to improve their hands as in regular Draw Poker, and there is a final round of betting.

Lowball

This is one of the most popular versions of Draw Poker, especially in the western United States. It is ideal for players who constantly complain about being dealt poor hands because in Lowball, the lowest hand wins the pot! The ace is always low, so that two aces are the lowest pair. It is optional to count or not count straights and flushes. If they don't count, the lowest possible hand is 5, 4, 3, 2, A, regardless of suits. This hand is called a "wheel" or a "bicycle" — named after *Bicycle* brand playing cards. If it is agreed that straights and flushes do count, then 6, 4, 3, 2, A is the lowest hand possible, though it is recommended that

Lowball should be played with the "wheel" as the lowest.

There are no minimum requirements for opening the pot, and after the draw, a player may check. The betting for this round always begins with the active player nearest the dealer's left.

A satisfactory Lowball hand is 9-high (such as 9, 7, 5, 4, A), and a good low hand is 8-high. It is rare for a good player to have to draw two or three cards; most of the time, the winner will have stayed pat or drawn just one card. (Lowball can also be played as a version of Stud Poker.)

Jacks to open – trips to win – once you get out, you can't get in

Play a normal hand of Draw Poker. To open the betting before the draw, a player must have a pair of jacks or better in his hand. If no one can open, players re-ante and a new round is dealt (some players do not require this re-ante; dealer should state his preference in advance). If a player opens the game, play proceeds as normal. When hands are revealed, if the highest player doesn't have a hand that is 3 of a kind or better, the hand is null, the players re-ante and another round is dealt. If a player folds, however, he is not dealt back in when a new round is dealt. Best hand that is 3 of a kind or better wins the pot.

Frankenstein

This is a normal 5-card draw game. However, when the cards are discarded for the draw, those cards are gathered up and form the "Frankenstein" hand, which is face down until the showdown. There is a betting round before and after the draw. If any player folds, they remain out of the game and are not dealt back in, in case of a new round. After the final round of betting, the best five-card hand among the players still in must also beat the Frankenstein hand, which is revealed and arranged by the dealer with input from all other players after the showdown. If the best hand beats the Frankenstein hand, that player wins the pot. If the Frankenstein hand is better than the winning hand, however, the pot remains unclaimed. Then, a new hand is dealt to all players who did not fold, and the process is repeated.

Color Poker

This game is a split the pot game where the winners will be based on the best hand in black cards, and the best hand in red cards. Deal each player four cards. There are three betting rounds, and after each of the first two rounds, players are dealt an additional two cards. After the final betting round, each player makes a hand of five cards. When the hands are revealed, the highest hand using only black cards, and the highest hand using only red cards split the pot.

Pip Poker

This game is a Five-Card Draw game where players can draw up to three cards as per normal. Instead of the best five-card hand deciding the winner, the person who has the most pips on their cards wins. Number cards count as the number (3 = 3 pips, 10 = 10 pips), face cards are zero pips, aces are one pip. Whichever player has the most pips wins.

Pregnant Three's

A normal Five-Card Draw game in which threes, sixes, and nines are wild. Best five-card hand wins.

Draw Poker with the Stripped Deck

This game is played with five or less players and can be played with 44 cards (twos and threes are removed), 40 cards (twos, threes, and fours are removed), or less by removing anywhere up to 20 cards (all twos through sixes). Aces rank just below the lowest value still remaining in the deck when they are viewed as low.

Six-Card Poker with Draw

This game can be played with five players (deuces are wild) or six players (deuces and jokers wild). Each player is dealt six cards and can discard and draw up to four replacement cards. The player with the best complete six-card hand wins. Hands are rated as follows: six of a kind, six straight flush, fours with a pair, double triplets, six flush, six straight, three pair.

BICYCLE
7

Stud Poker Games

Of the many variations of Stud Poker, the basic rules for which are defined on pages 49-55, following are currently the most popular variants.

Five-Card Stud

Two to ten people may play, though the game is best for five to eight players. There is no ante in some Five-Card Stud games, but the players agree in advance on the minimum that must be bet.

Not having an ante means that a person could turn down their first two cards on every deal, without ever contributing to the pot. The dealer gives each player one card face down, and then each one card face up. The player with the highest up card makes the first bet of at least the agreed-on minimum or else drops and turns down his up card. In any later betting interval, the first bettor and players after him may check, unless and until a bet is made.

The first bettor in each betting interval is the player with the highest Poker combination showing. If two or more players are tied for highest, the one nearest the dealer's left is the first bettor.

Following the first betting interval, the dealer gives another card face up to each active player in rotation; there is another betting interval, another round of face-up cards to the remaining active players, another betting interval, and then a final round of face-up cards and a final betting interval. Thus, each active player who is still in the game at the last round will have one card face down and four cards face up.

If two or more players remain after the final betting interval, there is a showdown in which each player turns up his hole card. If a bet or raise goes uncalled in any betting interval by all the other remaining players, the pot is taken by the bettor. Players who drop must immediately turn all of their cards face down.

It is the dealer's duty, after each round of cards is dealt, to designate the first bettor (as by saying, "First king bets," or "Pair of sixes bets"). In a very large game, if there are not enough cards left in the pack for a final round of dealing, the dealer may flash a card from the top of the pack (turn it face up on the table), and this card serves as the common fifth card for all the hands.

Last Card Down

This is regular Five-Card Stud, except that the fifth card dealt is face down instead of face up.

Hole Card Stud

This is a regular Five-Card Stud game, except the first card is dealt face down to each player followed by a betting round. The last four cards are dealt face up with betting after each round of face-up cards.

Last Card Optionally Down

This game is similar to standard Five-Card Stud, except that the player may turn up his hole card before the last round is dealt and ask for the fifth card to be dealt face down. It is standard to require the player requesting this change to match the original ante to "pay for" this privilege.

Mexican Stud

In this version of Five-Card Stud, the first two cards are dealt to each player face down. Players look at their cards and select one to be placed face up. The concealed card is then wild for each player. After a round of betting, another card is dealt around face down. Each player then decides which of the two concealed cards to turn face up, and which to keep face down for a wild card. Another round of betting follows. The process continues until each player has four cards exposed and one wild card concealed. This card is wild only for the player who holds it; also wild for that player are all other cards of the same rank as the concealed card. After the final round of betting, all players still in the game show their

concealed cards and announce the value of
their hands.

Seven-Card Stud

The game of Seven-Card Stud is extremely
popular, especially where the version of High-
Low Poker is played. In High-Low games, the
highest hand and the lowest hand split the pot.
Two to eight people may play, though the game
is best for at least five players. In the initial
deal, each player receives two cards face down
and then one card face up, all dealt one at a
time in rotation. There is then a betting interval, initiated by the player with the highest up
card. In case of a tie, the player closest to the
dealer's left with the highest up card initiates
the betting. Each active player receives three
more face-up cards and one more face-down
card, in that order, with a betting interval after
each round of cards that is dealt. In the showdown, each player turns up all his hole cards
and selects five of the seven cards as his hand.
The player must separate these five cards from
the other two, which he discards. The cards
then speak for themselves, as in any other form
of Poker, and the player may not reclaim his
two discards upon finding that a better five-
card combination could have been made. In

other respects the procedure is the same as in Five-Card Stud. When playing for both high and low, a player mentally selects two five-card hands from among the cards that he holds. There are two ways in which tied hands may be ruled, but before the game, the dealer must announce which way the game will be played. The first version states that if a player claims both high and low, and is tied or beaten on either, he loses any title to the pot. The second version states that if a player declares both high and low, he must at least tie each way or he receives nothing.

Seven-Card Stud – Deuces Wild

This game is the same as Seven-Card Stud except that deuces are wild. After the first up card is dealt, the player with a deuce closest to the dealer's left begins the betting. If no one has a deuce, the highest card begins the betting. After this betting round, the person with the highest up cards begins the betting.

Seven-Card Flip

Four face-down cards are dealt to each player. After examining them, the player turns up any two of the four. There is a betting interval, then play proceeds as in regular Seven-Card Stud. Three more cards are dealt, two up and one down, and there is a betting interval following each.

In another version, each player first receives two cards, one up and one down, followed by a betting interval; then another two cards, one up and one down, and another betting interval; then two cards a third time and a betting interval; then a seventh card face down. Each player then discards one face-down card and one face-up card, leaving a hand of three concealed cards and two exposed cards. The final betting interval and showdown follow.

Sevens Up

In this seven-card game, wild cards are deuces, one-eyed jacks (hearts and spades), and the man with the axe (king of diamonds). In the initial deal, each player receives two cards face down and then one card face up, all dealt one at a time in rotation. There is then a betting interval, initiated by the player with the highest up card. In case of a tie, the player closest to the dealer's left with the highest up card initiates the betting. Each active player receives three more face-up cards and one more face-down card, in that order, with a betting interval after each round of cards is dealt. In the showdown, each player turns up all of his hole cards and selects the best five-card Poker hand (with five wilds being the highest). The seven cards add a twist to this game. Whenever a player shows a "natural" pair of sevens (face-down cards can also be used, but wild cards do not count as sevens for this purpose), he takes the pot at that time because a pair of sevens is the automatic winning hand. If two players each have a pair of sevens, then the first one who shows these two cards claims the pot. A player with one or more sevens face down may delay showing his pair of sevens and claiming the pot until after several or even all rounds of betting if he so chooses. If no players have a pair of sevens, then the best five-card hand, including wild cards, wins the pot.

Baseball

This game is played like Seven-Card Stud, except nines are always wild and threes are wild when dealt as a hole card. If a three is dealt as an up card, the player must fold unless he is willing to match the pot. If the player matches the pot, he can keep the three as a

wild up card. If a player gets a four, that player gets an additional down card dealt out of
turn to them. (If the four is face down, the
player may turn it up and have the extra card
dealt – usually, the player must "purchase" this
extra card by adding an extra ante.) Best five-
card hand wins.

Night Baseball

This increasingly popular game may be
played with as many as nine cards per person
(Major League Night Baseball) or as few as six
(Little League Night Baseball). All threes and
nines are wild, and a player turning over a four
may purchase an additional card from the top
of the deck by adding an extra ante; he may
take this card up or down, placing it wherever
he wants in his card stack. Each player is dealt
all of his cards down at once. The players may
not look at their cards, although they may
shuffle them as desired without looking at
them. After all players ante, the player to the
dealer's left turns over his first card. He then
initiates a round of betting. The player to his
left then turns over as many cards as are needed to have a better Poker hand than the first
player, and then initiates another round of betting. This process continues, with each player

turning over cards one at a time until he has a better Poker hand than the previous player. Players must call bets in order to stay in the game, even if they have not had a chance to see any of their cards yet. After all the cards have been turned over, the player who has stayed in and has the best five-card Poker hand wins the pot.

Five-Card Baseball

This game is played as Five-Card Stud, but with the rules of baseball. A few additional rules are also included. If a nine or three is dealt as an up card, the player has to match the pot. When a player is dealt a four, the additional card must be dealt face up.

Football

This Seven-Card Stud game is played the same as Baseball, except that sixes and fours are wild. A four requires a player to match the pot or drop, and a deuce entitles a player to an extra hole card if he adds an extra ante.

Heinz

In this Seven-Card Stud game, fives and sevens are wild, but a player dealt one of these cards face up must match the pot or drop.

Woolworth

In this Seven-Card Stud game, fives and tens are wild. A player dealt a five face up must match the ante x 5 or drop, and a player dealt a ten face up must match the ante x 10 or drop.

Six-Card Stud

The first five cards are dealt as in regular Five-Card Stud, but after the fourth betting interval, each player receives a second hole card. This card becomes an alternate card and can replace any of the existing five. Then there is a final betting interval on the sixth card, and each player selects five of the six cards as his final hand.

Eight-Card Stud

The game is identical to Seven-Card Stud, except that each player receives an eighth card, dealt either up or down, as the dealer may decide in advance. After the eighth card is dealt, there is another betting round followed by players selecting their five-card hand.

Seven-Card No Peek

Each player is dealt seven cards face down. Players may not look at their cards. The first player to the left of the dealer turns up one card and then bets. All players must call or fold. This process continues, with each player turning over cards one at a time until he has a better Poker hand than the previous player. Players must call bets in order to stay in the game, even if they have not had a chance to see any of their cards yet. After all the cards have been turned over, the player who has stayed in and has the best five-card Poker hand wins the pot.

Five-Card No Peek

Identical to Seven-Card No Peek except that each player receives only five cards.

Bull

Each player receives three cards face down. Players arrange them in any order desired, but may not thereafter change the order. There is a betting interval. Then, each player receives four face-up cards, one at a time, with a betting interval after each. Next, each player turns up his first face-down card, followed by a betting interval, and then his second face-down card, followed by the final betting interval. The last card is then turned up for the showdown. The best five-card Poker hand wins the pot.

Follow the Queen

Deal two cards down and one up. Continue deal as if playing normal Seven-Card Stud with betting after every new card is dealt. If a queen is dealt as a face-up card, the next card dealt is wild, and all cards of that rank in all players' hands, whether up or down, are wild. If another queen is dealt as a face-up card, then the previous wild card is cancelled, and the next card dealt is wild, again for all players. Players may request that their last card be dealt face up, rather than face down, paying an extra ante for the privilege. If the last face-up card is a queen or no queens are dealt face up, then no cards are wild. The best five-card hand wins.

Queen and What Follows

This game is played the same as Follow the Queen, except that all queens are always wild plus the card that comes after the queen. If a second queen is dealt as a face-up card, then the previous wild card is cancelled, and the next card dealt after the queen is wild. Players may request that their last card be dealt face up, rather than face down, paying an extra ante for the privilege. If the last face-up card is a queen or no queens are dealt face up, then only queens are wild. The best five-card hand wins.

Deucey Trail

This game is played the same as Queen and What Follows, except that all twos are always wild and if a two is dealt as a face-up card, the next card dealt is wild, and all cards of that rank in all players hands, whether up or down, are wild. If another two is dealt as a face-up card, then the previous wild card is cancelled, and the next card dealt is wild, again for all players. Players may request that their last card be dealt face up, rather than face down, paying an extra ante for the privilege. If the last face-up card is a two or no twos are dealt face up, then only twos are wild. The best five-card hand wins.

Low Hole – Roll Your Own

In this version of Seven-Card Stud, the first three cards are dealt to each player face down. Players look at their cards and select one to be placed face up. The lowest concealed card is wild for each player—and only for that player; also wild for that player are all other cards of the same rank as the concealed card. After a round of betting, initiated by the player with the highest card showing, another card is dealt around face down. Each player then decides which one of the three concealed cards to turn face up. Another round of betting follows. The process continues until each player has four cards exposed and two cards concealed. The seventh card is then dealt to each player face down, unless a player makes a payment to the pot matching the ante to receive his card face up (thereby avoiding receiving a new, lower hole card that would then become wild). After the final round of betting, all players still in the game show their concealed cards and announce the value of their hands. Best five-card hand wins.

Black Mariah

This is a normal Seven-Card Stud game where all the queens are wild. If the queen of spades is dealt up to a player, then the round ends. Hands are dealt again, and play continues until there is no queen of spades drawn. If the queen of spades is a down card, it is merely a wild card.

Sailboats, Snowmen, and the Scourge

This is a normal Seven-Card Stud game where eights (snowmen), fours (sailboats), and the nine of diamonds (known as the scourge of Scotland because every ninth reagent of Scotland was known as a tyrant and the symbol of the Scottish reagent was a diamond) are wild. Best five-card hand wins.

Low-Ball

A normal Seven-Card Stud game where the lowest hand wins. Betting occurs after each round of cards being dealt past the third card.

Murder

A normal Seven-Card Stud game with the following exceptions. During any time in which a player is dealt a face-up card that matches another face up card he has, he must match the pot or fold. In addition, the player can then make a bet equal to the amount they matched, which all other players must then call or fold. Best five-card hand wins.

Klondike

In this Seven-Card Stud game, once per hand a player can discard one up card before the next card is dealt. A new card is dealt replacing the discarded card. The best five-card hand wins. Betting occurs after each card dealt past the third card.

Auction

A Seven-Card Stud game with the following addition: After each up card has been dealt, before the next card is dealt, any player may bid to take that card, and an auction may ensue among the players other than the original recipient of the card. The original recipient of the card at auction receives the value of the highest bid from the winning bidder, unless he pays into the pot the value of the highest bid of the auction to maintain the card. Best five-card hand wins.

Match the Hole Card

Five-Card or Seven-Card Stud Poker game in which any up card matched with a card of the same value in the hole makes both cards wild. Player with the best five-card hand wins. Betting occurs after each card dealt past the third card.

High Chicago

Five-Card or Seven-Card Stud Poker game in which the high five-card Poker hand and high spade in the hole (face down) split the pot. Betting occurs each deal after the third card. Best showing hand is the bettor.

Low Chicago

Five-Card or Seven-Card Stud Poker game in which the high five-card Poker hand and low spade in the hole (face down) split the pot. Betting occurs each deal after the third card. Best showing hand is the bettor.

Kings and Little Ones

In this Seven-Card Stud game, kings and the lowest value card (up or down) in your hand are wild. Once during the game prior to your last card down you may discard a card and replace it at a cost of four times the ante. Betting occurs after each card dealt past the third card. Highest five-card hand wins.

Low Card Wild

In this Seven-Card Stud game, a player's lowest card in the hole is wild. Other cards of the same value are also wild for the player. Best five-card hand wins. Betting occurs each deal after the third card. Player may purchase his last card up, rather than down, for 2x ante.

Seven-Card Blind End

In this Seven-Card Stud game, the seventh card is dealt to each player face down and the player cannot look at the card until it is turned over after all final bets have been called. The best five-card hand wins. Betting occurs after each card dealt past the third card.

Beat Charley

In this Five-Card Stud game, one card is dealt down to each player and one card up in the middle (Charley's hand). The player next to the dealer initiates a betting round. The next card is dealt down to all players and up to the middle hand. The second player to the left of the dealer then initiates a betting round. This process continues for five cards. The player with the highest Poker hand wins the pot if his winning hand is higher than Charley's. If not, all players who stayed in through the final round of betting ante again and the process is repeated. Any player who folds is out of the game for all subsequent deals of "Beat Charley," and cannot re-enter if the remaining players do not beat Charley.

Big Boys

This game is a Seven-Card No Peek game in which the highest showing card of every suit is wild; only that single card is wild, not all the cards of that rank. As players reveal new cards or drop out of the game, the wild cards readjust to be the highest of each suit; there are never more than four wild cards, and there can only be less than four if one or more suits never are revealed in the game. Each player is dealt seven cards down. The players may not look at their cards, although they may shuffle them as desired without looking at them. After all players ante, the player to the dealer's left turns over his first card. He then initiates a round of betting. The player to his left then turns over as many cards as are needed to have a better Poker hand than the first player, and then initiates another round of betting. This process continues, with each player turning over cards one at a time until he has a better Poker hand than the previous player. Players must call bets in order to stay in the game, even if they have not had a chance to see any of their cards yet. After all the cards have been turned over, the player who has stayed in and has the best five-card Poker hand wins the pot.

Six-Card Poker

This version of Six-Card Stud is played with twos wild, and jokers can also be included as wild cards. In this game, all six cards must be used. Rank of hands is as follows: six of a kind, six straight flush, fours with a pair, double triplets, six flush, six straight, three pair.

Sixty-Eight Stud

This game can be played with up to six players where both twos and jokers are wild. Deal each player two cards down and one card up followed by the first betting round. Deal four more up cards to each player, each followed by a round of betting. Then deal each player one down card before the final round of betting. Each player turns down two cards and the best complete six-card hand wins.

Seven-Card Poker

This game is ideal for six players and requires a 54-card deck, with twos and jokers being wild. Each player is dealt nine cards face down. After a round of betting, each player selects his seven best cards and the best seven-card hand wins. Rank of hands is as follows: seven of a kind, seven straight flush, five of a kind with a pair, 4 & 3 of a kind, seven flush, seven straight, three of a kind with two pair.

Seventy-Nine Stud

This game can be played with up to six players using a 54-card deck, with twos and jokers being wild. Deal each player two cards down and one card up. This is followed by a round of betting. Deal each player four more up cards, betting after each deal. Next, deal two down cards, each followed by a round of betting. Each player then selects a complete seven-card hand.

Four-Card Poker

Deal four cards to each player. After a round of betting, the best four-card hand wins. Rank of hands is as follows: four of a kind, straight flush, three of a kind, flush, straight, two pair, pair, ace high.

Three-Card Poker

Deal three cards to each player. After a round of betting, the best three-card hand wins. Rank of hands is as follows: straight flush, three of a kind, flush, straight, pair, ace high.

Two-Card Poker

Deal two cards to each player. After a round of betting, the best two-card hand wins. The highest possible hand consists of two aces. Two-card flushes and straights do not count.

One-Card Poker

Deal one card to each player. After a round of betting, the player with the highest card wins.

BICYCLE

8

"Common Card" Games

Of increasing popularity, particularly in larger Poker games, are "common card" games, in which all players share the opportunity to incorporate a certain number of common cards into their hole cards to form the best Poker hand. Following are the most popular current common card games, which use the same rank of hands as regular Draw and Stud Poker games.

Mambo Stud

Players are dealt one card up and one card down, then there is a round of betting. Next, each player gets one more card face up, followed by a betting round. Finally, a communal card is turned up in the center of the table to form the fourth card in the hand. This is a high-low game where the high hand and the low hand split the pot. Hand progressing goes as follows: high card, pair, two pair, three of a kind, four of a kind. Aces may be either high or low. Flushes and straights do not count in this and most four-card games.

Box

Deal each player two cards face down. A round of betting is initiated by the player to the dealer's left. Then deal an eight-card square of cards face-down, three cards on a side. Each player will be able to use the two cards in their hand and the three cards on any one side of the box to form a five-card hand. After the first betting round, the cards in two opposite corners of the box are revealed, and a round of betting follows, initiated by the player that initiated the previous round of betting. After this second betting round, the other two corner cards are revealed and a round of betting follows, initiated by the player that initiated the previous round of betting. After this third betting round, the four remaining cards are all revealed at once. Then there is a final round of betting and then hands are revealed. Highest five-card hand wins.

Cincinnati

Five cards are dealt to each player, followed by another hand of five cards face down on the table. A round of betting is initiated by the player on the dealer's left. The five center cards are turned up one at a time, with a round of betting each time a card is exposed. Each player selects a hand of five cards from among the cards in his own hand and the five on the table. Unless otherwise stated, flushes and straights may not use more than three cards from the common cards.

Cincinnati Liz

This game is the same as Cincinnati, but the lowest of the five common cards is wild, and all cards of that rank in players' hands are also wild.

Utah

This game is the same as Cincinnati, but the last card turned over from the five common cards is wild, and all cards of that rank in players' hands are also wild.

Hollywood

This game is the same as Cincinnati, but two rows of five cards each are dealt to the center face down. Center cards can either be turned up one at a time or in pairs (one from each row). Each person then has fifteen cards to choose from for their hand of five.

Texas Hold 'Em

In recent years, this game has become very popular in casinos that have Poker rooms. It is considered by many to require more skill than any other version of Poker. Each player receives two cards face down, and five cards are dealt face down to the center of the table. After the first betting interval, three of the five center cards are turned face up in the center. Then there is a second betting interval, followed by one more center card being turned up. Then there is a third betting interval, and the last center card is turned up. Next, there is a final betting round. The player must use his best five cards, taken from the two in his hand and the five turned up in the center of the table.

Omaha (7 card)

This game is similar to Hold 'Em, and it is also very popular in American casinos with a Poker room. Each player receives two cards face down and five cards are dealt to the center of the table. There is a betting interval, and the center cards are turned up one by one, with a betting interval after each card is exposed. All players still in the game must make hands of five cards using one or two cards from their own hand plus three or four from the five cards in the center. The best five-card hand wins the pot.

Omaha (9 card)

Each player is dealt four cards face down. A round of betting ensues. Then three cards are turned up in the center of the table followed by another betting round. Then one card is turned up in the center of the table, followed by another betting round. Then one final card is turned up in the center of the table. After the final betting round, the players make their best five-card hand from the five communal cards and their own four cards. When forming the hand, each player must use exactly two of the four hole cards and three of the five common cards to form his five-card hand. Highest five-card hand wins.

High-Low Omaha

Identical to Seven-Card Omaha, except that the best and the worst five-card hands split the pot. Unless otherwise stated, a qualifier of eight or better (that is, a hand with no pairs and a high card of eight or lower) is needed for a hand to be in contention for the low half of the pot. Otherwise, the high hand takes the entire pot.

Amarillo

This game is the same as Seven-Card Omaha, except that each player must use the two face-down cards and exactly three of the common cards to form his five-card hand.

444

Deal four cards to each player plus one extra four-card hand face down in the center. All fours are wild. After betting, turn over one card from the center hand, and a round of betting follows, initiated by the player that made the first bet in the previous round. Repeat the process three more times until all cards in the common hand are turned over. The best five-card hand, including any number of common cards, wins.

Crossover

Deal each player five cards face down, then deal the center five cards in cross formation. Center cards are turned over in the following order: left, top, right, bottom, center. There is a round of betting after the initial deal and then after each card is turned over. Instead of all five cards being a part of the player's hand, each person can only choose one row, either vertical or horizontal. Therefore, each player will have a choice from the five cards in his hand and three cards from the center to form the best five-card hand.

Criss Cross

This game is the same as Crossover with the center card, and all others of the same rank, wild.

Iron Cross

This game is the same as Crossover, except that each player's lowest card and all cards of that value are wild for him.

Nine-Card Crossover

This game is the same as Crossover, except there are nine center cards instead of five. This way, each player has five extra cards in addition to the five in his hand to choose from.

Fiery Cross

This Crossover game is played high/low and there are no wild cards. The high hand and the low hand share the pot. There are three ways in which this game can be played: 1) Each player has a high and low hand made with either or the same row of the cross. 2) Each player must make up their low hand with one row and their high hand with the second row of the cross. 3) Each player announces whether they are going for a high hand, low hand, or both. Players must also decide if high and low hands can come from the same row or not.

Bedsprings

Deal each player five down cards, then deal ten cards face down in two columns of five. The cards in the two columns are turned up one at a time with betting on each card. Then, each player chooses two side-by-side cards in the columns to add to their hand, enabling each player to make the best five-card hand from seven cards.

Twin Beds

Cards are dealt the same as in Bedsprings. Turn the top card of each column up and follow this with a round of betting. Next, turn the second card of each column up and follow with a round of betting. Continue this until all ten cards are turned over. Each player can choose one card from each of the columns to add to their hand, enabling each player to make the best five-card hand from seven cards.

Twin Beds Gone Wild

Cards are dealt the same as in Bedsprings. The top card of each column is wild along with all other cards of the same values. Each player can choose one card from each of the columns to add to their hand, but only one of the wild cards, enabling each player to make the best five-card hand from seven cards.

Seven-Card Common

Deal each player two down cards, then deal one card face up which serves as everyone's first up card. After betting, three more mutual up cards are dealt, each being followed by a round of betting. Next, deal each player one down card (the seventh card) and end with a round of betting. Each player then shows their best five cards, combining his three down cards with the four common up cards to make the best five-card hand.

Round the World

Deal four cards to each player, then deal a single card face up in the center (this is the common card that acts as the fifth card for all players). This is followed by a round of betting and then another card is dealt face up in the center. Repeat after betting by dealing two more common cards face up. The best five-card hand made from the four hand cards and the four common cards wins.

Spit in the Ocean

Deal four cards to each player. The next card in the pack is turned face up in the center of the table and it is considered to be the fifth card in each player's hand. After a betting interval, there is a draw as in standard Draw Poker, except that each player draws to a four-card hand. A player may draw up to four cards, discarding an identical number of cards from his hand first. After a final betting interval, there is a showdown.

Spit in the Ocean – Wild

Identical to Spit in the Ocean, except that the common up card is wild for all players, as are any cards of the same rank in players' hands.

Spit in the Ocean – Selective

Identical to Spit in the Ocean – Wild, except that the dealer places three up cards in the center of the table, and each player may select only one of these cards to be the fifth card in his hand and to be Wild, along with any other cards of the same rank in the player's hand.

The Wild Widow

Deal each player five cards face down, then deal a single card face up in the center which will be the wild value for that deal. However, this card is not wild, but all other cards of that value are wild. This means that there are three wild cards for every hand dealt. Continue play as in Draw Poker, limiting each player to a draw of three cards, unless a player shows an ace, in which case he is entitled to draw four cards.

Heaven & Hell (also known as "Bingo" or "Yahtzee")

Each player is dealt five cards face down. Players may pick up and review their cards, and a round of betting is initiated by the player to the dealer's left. Then two rows of five cards each are dealt face down on the table. Cards from these rows are turned up two a time, one from each row, with a betting round to follow each turn. The upper row of cards are common and may be used by each player to complete his hand, but as cards in the lower row are turned up, players must immediately discard all cards in their hand that match the value of these cards. Following the last round of betting, players must declare high/low/both. The high hand is the best five-card Poker hand, in which the player may use any combination of hand and common cards. The low hand is not the low Poker hand, but rather the lowest point count in each player's remaining hand, excluding the cards which were discarded. For point count, aces are worth one point and face cards are worth ten.

Supermarket (also known regionally by individual chain names, such as Kmart, Valu-Mart, etc.)

Each player is dealt one card face down, and three cards (A, B, C) are dealt face up near the stock. Beginning with the player on the dealer's left, in turn, each player may elect to take one of the three face-up cards (A, B or C), or the top card (D) from the stock, which is not exposed if taken. The player's choice of cards has financial implications: the cards have different unit prices based on the ante (x): A=3x, B=2x, C=1x, D=0. In other words, if a player wants the exposed card in stack A, he must pay three antes into the pot to take the card. If a player selects an exposed card, card D is turned over and placed in the most expensive exposed slot, and other exposed cards are bumped, if necessary, into the next cheapest slot. A round of betting is initiated by the player on the dealer's left after the dealer secures his second card. Subsequent betting rounds are initiated after the dealer secures each additional card, initiated by the player who initiated the betting in the previous round. The game is best played as a seven-card game, with a high/low/both declaration, and the pot split between the best and worst five-card Poker hands. For the low hand, aces are high, and straights and flushes are undesirable; the best low hand is 7-5-4-3-2 in multiple suits.

BICYCLE
9

Miscellaneous Poker Games

There are a number of great Poker games that do not fit neatly in a category. The best and most common of these are presented in this section.

Straight Poker

This may be the original form of Poker. Each player is dealt five cards face down. The players bet, and then there is a showdown; the best five-card hand wins. There is no draw in this version.

Cold Hands

In this version of Straight Poker, each player puts up an agreed ante. Five cards are then dealt to each player one at a time, face up, and the highest hand takes the pot. There is no draw and there are no rounds of betting.

Screw Your Neighbor

In this game, players do not ante and bet on individual hands, but rather put up initial stakes in the form of three equal "stacks" of chips. The loser(s) of each hand put(s) one stack into the pot, until only one player is left with one or more stacks. That player is the winner, and then takes all the stacks in the pot.

The object of this game is to avoid having the highest card in each round. Kings are the lowest cards in this game, followed by twos up through queens, and aces are the highest. Each player is dealt one card. The player to the left of the dealer looks at his card and decides whether or not to exchange cards with the person to the left. If a player decides to exchange, the player on his left must exchange cards with him, unless that player has a king, in which case the player shows the king to the active player and the switch doesn't take place. (In some games, it is deemed good form to display the king with great flourish and a loud "Quack!") The turn then goes to the player to the left of the player with the king, who then decides whether or not to exchange with the player on his left. This process is repeated by each player until it is the dealer's turn. The dealer then has the option of keeping his card (which may be his original card or the one he ended up with after the player to his right required him to switch with her) or exchanging it with the top card of the deck. Then all players reveal their cards. Whoever has the highest card puts one of their stacks into the pot; if there is a tie for the high card, all players with the highest card put in their stack. The dealer then deals another round, but begins with the next person to the left, so that the opportunity for the first exchange, and for the final exchange with the deck, rotates one player to the left with each deal. When a player loses the last of his three stacks, he is out of the game.

Three-Card Monty

This game is a high/low game where each winner splits half the pot. It is dealt one card up, one card down, then one card up. There are betting rounds after each card is dealt. After the third betting round each player may choose to pay an additional ante in order to discard one card and draw a new one. The replacement card is dealt in the same manner as the discarded card (face up/down). In this game, there are no straights or flushes (Three of a kind is the best hand, followed by a pair and then high card).

Indian Poker

This is one-card Poker, with an interesting twist. A single card is dealt face down to each player. On a signal from the dealer, each player simultaneously lifts his card, placing it on his forehead so that all of the other players can see it, but the player cannot see his own. There is a single round of betting and then a showdown, which, at times, can be quite hilarious. In some games the suits have rank - spades (high), hearts, diamonds, clubs - so that the ace of spades would be the highest card, the ace of hearts the next highest, and so on.

Knock Poker

This game is for three to five players. Each

player antes one chip, and the dealer gives each player five cards as in Draw Poker. The undealt cards are placed in the center to form the stock. The player to the dealer's left draws the top card and then discards one card face up; thereafter each player in turn may draw the top card of the stock or the last previous discard, as in various games of Rummy, and then discard one card into the discard pile.

Any player, after drawing and before discarding, may knock. He does so by knocking on the table and discarding. Then each other player has one turn to draw and discard until play comes back to the knocker, who does not have another turn. Each player, after drawing, may either drop out, immediately paying the knocker the equivalent of the ante, or he may stay in.

When the last player before the knocker has drawn and discarded, there is a showdown among all who have stayed in. If the knocker has the high hand, each player who stayed in pays the successful knocker an amount equal to the pot. If another player ties the knocker, they divide the winnings except for chips paid to the knocker by the players who dropped out. If the knocker does not have the high hand, he pays an ante to every player who stayed in and pays the player with the high hand an amount equal to the pot. All players re-ante and the dealer deals another hand, beginning the deal and the play with the next player to the left. Hands are played in the same fashion, with each deal rotating one player to the left, until no players stay in with the knocker. The unchallenged knocker then collects the pot and the game ends.

Knock Poker bonuses for the winner are popular but they need not be used unless the players agree. If there is a bonus, everyone pays it, even a player who has dropped. Popular bonuses include two antes for knocking and winning without drawing a card; four antes for winning with a royal flush; two antes for winning with any other straight flush; one ante for winning with four of a kind.

Whiskey Poker

After an ante from all players, the dealer gives five cards, face down, to each player and puts an extra hand ("widow") of five cards face down in the middle of the table. He must deal to each player in turn around to the left, one card at a time, then to the widow, then to himself last. Beginning with the player to the dealer's left, each player has the option of exchanging his hand for the widow, or keeping his hand as it is. If a player takes up the widow, his original five cards are placed face up on the table and become the new widow. Each player in turn has the option of taking up one to five cards of the new widow and replacing it with an equal number of cards from his hand. If a player wishes to play the original hand, he signals by knocking on the table at his turn rather than exchanging with the widow.

The process of exchanging cards continues around the table until a player knocks, after which each player has only one more chance to exchange cards. No player may draw if he has knocked. A player may knock before the widow is exposed, if desired. If no one takes the widow until it comes around to the dealer, the dealer must either take up the widow or turn it face up on the table. Even if the dealer knocks, and does not take up the widow, he must spread it on the table for each player to see and draw once more. A player may pass at any turn - that is, decline either to exchange or to knock; however, he may not pass at two turns in a row. Having passed on the previous round, he must either exchange or knock. After the knock and the final round of draws, all hands are shown, and the highest takes the pot. Some players require the lowest hand to match the pot, so that the winner receives the antes plus an additional sum equal to the antes. Others prefer to have a round of betting immediately before the showdown.

Red and Black

Strictly speaking, this game is not a form of Poker, but it is often played for variety during some social Poker games. In this game, each player is playing against the dealer, who acts as the banker for this game. Each player in turn, beginning on the dealer's left, places any bet up to the limit, and names "red" or "black." The dealer gives the player five cards face up. If three or more are of the color named, the dealer pays the bet; if three or more are of the opposite color, the dealer collects the bet. If all five cards are of the same color, double the bet is paid or collected.

Three-Card Guts

Each player antes and then is dealt three cards. There is no betting. Beginning with the player to the dealer's left, each player must state whether he is in or out. When the first player declares that he is in, all players then have one chance to declare whether they are in or out, even if they have previously declared themselves out. All players staying in then reveal their cards, and the best three-card hand wins the pot. The losing players must each match the pot; house rules may limit the size of the matched pot to 3-5x the total ante, but all players must agree to that limit before the first hand is dealt. The dealer then deals another hand to all players in the same fashion, but beginning with the player to the left of the previous first player. This new first player then begins the "in or out" declaration phase of the game. This process repeats, with the first player rotating one spot to the left each deal, until only one player stays "in;" that player then collects the pot and the game is over. Guts can also be played where there is a blind hand that players must beat or all players must match the pot.

Four-Two Exchange

Each player antes and then is dealt four cards. There is no betting. Beginning with the player to the dealer's left, each player must state whether he is in or out. When the first player declares that he is in, all players then have one chance to declare whether they are in or out, even if they have previously declared themselves out. All players declaring themselves out at this point are out for the duration of the game, including subsequent deals. All players staying in can discard zero, one or two cards and receive an equal number of new cards. Following the draw, beginning with the first player who declared he was in during the initial round, each player who stayed in for the draw must state whether he is in or out for the showdown. When the first player declares that he is in, all players who stayed in for the draw then have one chance to declare whether they are in or out for the showdown, even if they have previously declared themselves out in that round. All players declaring themselves out at this point must pay an additional ante for the privilege. All players declaring themselves in then reveal their cards, and the best four-card hand wins the pot (flushes and straights do not count unless previously agreed otherwise). The losing players must each match the pot; house rules may limit the size of the matched pot to 3-5x the total ante, but all players must agree to that limit before the first hand is dealt. The dealer then deals another hand to all players who remained in after the first round of the preceding deal in the same fashion, but beginning with the player to the left of the previous first player. This new first player then begins the "in or out" declaration phase of the game. This process repeats, with the first player rotating one spot to the left each deal, until only one player stays "in" during the final round; that player then collects the pot and the game is over.

High/Low Poker

Can be played in virtually any Poker version, including Stud and Draw. When the hands are finally declared, the player with the highest hand splits the pot with the player who holds the lowest hand. In a game involving more than five cards, players may declare for both high and low in an effort to win the entire pot. When playing for both high and low, a player mentally selects two five-card hands from among the cards that he holds. There are two ways in which tied hands may be ruled, but before the game, the dealer must announce which way the game will be played. The first version states that if a player claims both high and low, and is tied or beaten on either, he loses any title to the pot. The second version states that if a player declares both high and low, he must at least tie each way or he receives nothing.

Pass the Trash

Deal seven cards to each player. Each player selects three cards that he wants the least and places them face down in front of them. After each player has downed three cards, they push (give) them to the player on their left to add to their hand. Betting occurs before and after the push. The best five-card hand wins.

Take It or Leave It

Deal one card down followed by one card up to each player. When the face-up card is dealt to the player on the dealer's left, that player can choose to keep it or push (give) the card to the player on his left and be dealt a new card, which he must then keep. The second player can push or keep the card she received. The deal continues until all players have one up card in addition to their down card. If the dealer pushes a card, it is discarded and he must then keep the next card dealt to him. There is a round of betting after all players have received an up card. Repeat until all players have five cards, four up and one down. The best five-card hand wins.

Shove Them Along

This game is the same as Take It or Leave It, but instead a player may push along any one up card at his turn, rather than only the one just dealt.

In-Between (Acey Deucey)

Each player antes. One at a time, each player gets two cards face up and must decide if the rank of a third card will lie between the first two. An ace must be called high or low by the player if it is the first card. If an ace is dealt as the second card, it is always high. The player may pass without penalty, in which case his two cards are collected and the dealer moves to the next player on the left, or the player may wager any amount up to the pot (maximum bet first round is double the ante) that the value of the third card will lie in-between the value of his first two cards. If the value of the third card is in between the first two cards, the player takes the amount of his wager from the pot; if the value of the card is not between the first two cards, the player must put the amount of his wager into the pot. If the third card matches either of the two up cards, the player must pay double the amount

119

he bet. If the player wins on a bet for the pot, the game is over. OPTION: If a player is dealt two matching cards, he must re-ante.

7/27

The player with cards that total closest to 7 splits the pot with the player closest to 27. Aces can be 1 or 11, face cards are 1/2, and all other cards are at face value. Each player is dealt two cards, one face down, the other face up. Betting occurs. Players then have an option of taking another face up card or passing. Under beats over if tied, unless previously agreed on otherwise, but ties at the same number are not broken and thus split their share of the pot. Betting occurs each deal after the first up card, and there is no limit to the number of cards a player may take. When no player takes a card, the betting is over. A player may attempt to bluff in the beginning by not taking a card and then take a card toward the end of the game; some players have adopted a rule that permits players to only pass on taking a card three times before they are no longer allowed to take a card, but this rule is not recommended. After the betting is completed, players simultaneously declare they are going for 7, 27 or both. If a player declares for both, there are two ways in which tied hands may be ruled, but before the game, the dealer must announce which way the game will be played. The first version states that if a player declares both high and low, and is tied or beaten on either, he loses any title to the pot. The second version states that if a player declares both high and low, he must at least tie each way or he receives nothing.

BICYCLE
10

Poker Ethics
and Strategy

Poker Ethics

The only safe guiding principle in Poker ethics is, "When in Rome, do as the Romans do." "House rules" are therefore always important to clarify up front. In some games, a player may do anything to fool the opponents as long as he does not cheat. It is considered part of the skill of the game to bluff and mislead opponents, and by no means unsportsmanlike. In some games, it is considered unethical, or at least "sharp practice," to check while holding a good hand in the hope that someone else will bet and the player can raise him. Since card playing is a social pastime, a player is best advised to learn and follow the standards of the other players involved in the game.

Bluffing. To bluff in Poker is to make a bet on a hand the player knows, or believes, is not the best, in the hope that other players will believe his cards are strong and will fold. Bluffing is so much a part of Poker that the game would be incomplete without it. But some players believe their opponent should not support the bluff by making remarks he knows are untrue, such as announcing his hand has improved in the draw when it has not.

Intentionally Breaking the Rules. In most circles it is not considered ethical to announce, out of turn, an intention to bet, raise, or fold, if there is no intention of doing so when the player's turn comes. Although such false announcements are not formally penalized, regard for the other players should rule them out when they conflict with the code of ethics followed in the game. It is always considered unethical to intentionally break the rules.

Splitting Pots. In all Poker circles it is considered unethical, and close to cheating, for two or more players to agree to split a pot without showing their hands rather than have a show-down.

Betting Blind. When a player announces that he is betting (or checking) "blind," (that is, without looking at his hand), it is considered unethical if the player has, in fact, seen his hand.

Poker Strategy

The following pointers represent a general strategy for playing Poker based on mathematical likelihoods and odds. Players who like to play "hunches" may disregard at their risk!

How a player should evaluate a hand in a 5-card draw, no wild card seven player game:

-If dealt a straight or better, a player should bet or raise even if two others have already raised. The chances of winning the pot are very high.

-If dealt three of a kind, a player should raise even if one other has already done so. However, if two have already raised, the player should call.

-If dealt two pairs, a player should raise immediately. Chances are 11 to 1 that a player will not improve their hand in the draw. Raising may cause players to fold their hands when they might have stayed and improved.

-If dealt a pair of aces, a player should open the pot and stay even if others raise the pot.

-If dealt a pair of kings and five or six players remain OR dealt a pair of queens and four players remain, a player should open the pot, but drop if the pot is raised.

-If a player is one of the last three to make a bet (all others have checked), only do so on a pair of jacks or better.

-If another player opens the pot, one should not stay in unless holding a pair of queens or better. However, one may want to stay if four or five players have stayed in and it doesn't seem that anyone else will raise or if one is holding a straight or flush possibility.

-If a player holds a four flush, the flush should be dropped unless the pot has four times the amount that the player put in. This is because the odds against completing the flush are more than four to one when drawing one card.

-If a player holds a double ended straight (ex: 4-5-6-7), the cards should be dropped unless the pot has five times the amount the player put in (odds against completing the straight are 5 to 1).

-If a player holds a straight that only one card rank can complete, such as A-K-Q-J or 9-8-6-5, the odds against drawing the needed card to complete the "inside straight" are 11 to 1 and the player should not stay in if others have bet.

How a player should handle the draw in Draw Poker:

-When holding a pair or three of a kind, a player should hold only those cards and draw for the others. However, when holding three of a kind, one may want to draw only one card when it seems another player may have two high pairs.

-If a player is dealt a four-card straight and a pair (odds against a straight are 4-to-1) or a four flush and a pair (odds against a flush are 5-to-1), it is best to draw to the pair unless the pot is large enough to match the odds. A player should only draw one card if there is a four-card straight or flush possibility.

How a player should evaluate a hand in Stud Poker:

-If a player's hand is beaten by the face up cards of anyone else, that player should drop out.

-If a player has a concealed pair, betting should be done immediately. In the case of an open pair, the player should bet the limit immediately. This is done as long as there are no visible higher pairs.

How a player should evaluate a hand in Deuces Wild (Draw Poker):

-If a player holds a deuce or a pair of aces, he should open.

-If a player holds two low pairs, he should open if he is one of the last two players and all others have checked. Otherwise, the player should split or throw away the low pair.

-Unless the player has at least three aces (including a deuce) or a pair of deuces, he should not raise before the draw.

-If a player holds two deuces, draw three cards. However, if the player also holds an ace, keep it and only draw two cards.

Chances of Improving a Hand on the Draw (with no wild cards):

Drawing Four Cards to an Ace

A pair of aces or better	1 in 4
Two pairs or better	1 in 12

Drawing Three Cards to a Pair

Two pairs	1 in 6
Three of a kind	1 in 9
Full house	1 in 100
Four of a kind	1 in 350

Drawing Two Cards to a Pair and an Ace Kicker

Two pairs	1 in 6
Three of a kind	1 in 13
Full house	1 in 120
Four of a kind	1 in 1100

Drawing Two Cards to Three of a Kind

Full house	1 in 16
Four of a kind	1 in 23

Drawing One Card to Three of a Kind

Full house	1 in 15
Four of a kind	1 in 47

Drawing One Card to a Four-flush

Flush	1 in 5

Drawing One Card to Two Pairs

Full House	1 in 11

Drawing One Card to an Open-ended Straight (e.g., 5,6,7,8; need a 4 or a 9)

Straight	1 in 5

Drawing One Card to an Inside Straight (e.g., 5,6,8,9; need a 7)

Straight	1 in 11

These tables are adopted from *"The Complete Guide to Winning Poker"* by Albert H. Morehead (1967, Simon & Schuster).